RON BLOCK

DISMAL RIVER

A Narrative Poem with
pictures by Gaylord Schanilec

Minnesota Voices Project Number 38

NEW RIVERS PRESS 1990

Some of the poems in *Dismal River* originally appeared (sometimes in dif-
ferent versions) in *Prairie Schooner, New Letters, Iowa Review,* and *Epoch*. One
of his ballades from *Dismal River* was included in Philip Dacey's anthology,
Strong Measures: Contemporary Poetry in Traditional Forms. Grateful
acknowledgement is given to the editors of these publications for permis-
sion to reprint them here.

The publication of *Dismal River* has been made possible by grant support
from the Jerome Foundation, the First Bank System Foundation, the Arts
Development Fund of the United Arts Council, and the National Endow-
ment for the Arts (with funds appropriated by the Congress of the United
States). New Rivers Press also wishes to thank the Minnesota Non-Profits
Assistance Fund (a program of the Minneapolis Foundation) for its timely
and generous support.

New Rivers Press books are distributed by

The Talman Company
150-5th Avenue
New York, NY
10011

Dismal River has been manufactured in the United States of America for
New Rivers Press (C. W. Truesdale, Editor/Publisher), 420 North 5th
Street/Suite 910, Minneapolis, MN 55401 in a first edition of 1,200 copies.

For My Mother and My Father

DISMAL RIVER

CROSSING OVER

DOWN THE DISMAL RIVER

TO THE RIVER'S MOUTH

NEBRASKA

Bad neighborhoods don't scare me nearly as much
as the middle of nowhere; the flatlands make me want
to grab at fences to keep from floating off.
Irradiated, the grass pulls out like hair
by handfulls. The ghosts of thistles roll about
in the afterlife of tumbleweeds,
a retarded prophesy of the drought last year,
until barbed wire catches them trying to escape.

A dizzy jaybird sings for the flat, flat land,
a sympathetic monotone. The highest spot
on earth, a fence post, loses balance, leans.
—Even gripping to the steering wheel
doesn't offer much to hang on to. The cross wind
catches a canoe strapped upside down on the cab.
I'm traveling Nebraska on two wheels.
The only thing that keeps me from toppling over
is the thought, Where would I topple into
in the middle of nowhere? Would I fall,
like a body struggling to stay awake,
back into myself with a jerk?
Would I grow weightless as a body in despair?

The road erodes. Grass rises up to rub
the underbelly of Foster's truck until it submits,
and I grip the steering wheel with both hands
just to keep the pickup shivering in place.

FOSTER
AND THE
OTHER

With his boots on the dash, Foster appears
to be sleeping until he says, "Where are we?"

Nebraska.
      "Nebraska?"
              Nebraska.
"Yeah, but where in Nebraska?"
                      I don't know,
I thought "Nebraska" would be close enough.

"You have to get back on the main road," he says
and takes his own advice, going back to sleep.

After the main road goes abstract with the miles,
the aging of the land picks up its pace.
The prehistoric sea dries up, the fields
contract and wrinkle, aging before our eyes.
A mirage travels the road ahead of me.
Waves of sand-dunes crest and echo out.
We're already in a capsized boat.

Above our heads, and bouyed by fear, a hard
blue sky fills up with clouds like clouds
of sperm a little bloody in the east,
and we sink down towards the Dismal River,
tilted above a buckled road.

Foster says, "For us to be getting down this river
I'm going to have to invent a bit, but you'll
never know what I'll be inventing. I could say
the farmers plant a straight line by keeping their eyes
on a far point, say the state capitol, or like Brady,
say it's been so hot you can piss at your foot and not
get it wet. On a calm night you can hear the town's pulse,
four beats a minute. And when it's clear you can see
Cheyenne oil fires. Today, back in town, a cloud passed over.
People stood looking at the sky for several minutes,
and the old people talked of it for hours.
Sometimes the pulse gets down to three beats a minute,
and the old people come out and waltz."

I

                      "I was sitting
in a bar where two Indians were keeping play
at a pool table, winning — it was a territory
they could fight for — drunk and winning.
The one dropped a red-striped fifteen by accident,
smiled at the other and said, 'I'll take that,'
while the other, his eyes focused on some spot
not quite in the room, not quite within a few blocks
of here, leaned on his cue. After a few beers,
I went to see a man about a horse,
as Brady would say, and in the can I began
to think about what the phrase could mean.
Maybe some horse-trading turned into a piss-
poor deal, or maybe traders found agreement
by a handshake, smoke, spit of chaw,
and a friendly piss, standing by the field's edge,
putting down their x's in the dirt."

"Then it hit me that the phrase could come
from the Sioux twilight when the whites were confident
the Sioux would sell the most of their horses as
winter set in, their beef rations halved,
them dying liquored to be rubbed out smooth, and they
prepared for the end so that the Apache
stopped shooting their horses and tearing their arms at death
and tried to be glad for death, and among the Crow
the women came into the dance circle with the men,
some tribes dancing unclothed as in that death
where they could be equal and glad, as in the great
Ghost Dance that Jack Wilson started by the stockade,
foreseeing that the world would be destroyed
and recreated a larger space. Then among
the Sioux who modestly danced with bits of cloth
connecting men's and women's hands, whose last hope
of unity with the past and each other was the dance
that scared the army so the Hotchkiss guns
began to drum the air — they danced until
a mass-grave peace was made, the few left
starving so that going to see a man
about a horse became known to be as easy
as pissing."

I

"And I started laughing, not hard,
not really at anything but my own concoction
while standing too drunk too long in the pisser,
connecting my dick with a horse with an Indian Jesus,
connecting death with the dick and the gods with the dick.
I couldn't help it, I cracked-up and didn't know
the other Indian with the distant stare
was standing behind me, thinking I was laughing —
I don't know — at him. He asked, 'Sompin funny?'
I don't mean to give him a sixth sense
if my story robs him of the other five,
but his eyes were focused somewhere behind my head,
and it shook me up the way he looked through me,
and I said, because I thought he'd miss the joke,
'You know that codger Brady Tucker? No? Well,
I was standing here the other night and he
came in here and said, "Hey you put that thing down,
you don't know where it's been,"' but the Indian
said to me, now staring at me, 'Sompin funny, *Sioux?*'
(Brady told me later that the Indian was railroad
Chippewa and his calling me a *Sioux*
was as bad, in his mind, as calling me
a rabbit-choker.) I said, 'Nothing's funny, Jack,'
and saw a burst of white, an explosion that diffused
into a dozen white spots, floating over my eyes.
As the Indian picked me up by my collar, he said,
'Hey, man, don't fuck with our gods.'"

"After getting most
of the blood off, I went into the bar again,
half-expecting to see the two Indians.
They were gone. Instead I saw Brady Tucker
who waved me over. 'Gechurself over here,' he says.
'I'm telling lies aboucha. Whacha need, a Blue?
Say you look like your woman's been sandpaperin'
yer ass.' He wore a cap that advertised
his favorite agri-business, one with a corncob
sailing on wings, and said, 'Foster here's got
himself a new pair of glasses. Double pane.
Thermal ones. Keep the cold out and the heat in,
right Foster? Thick sons-a-bitches. Anyways,
he was in the head just now with those
magnifying glasses of his, admirin' that big
bastard in his hand, and the small one done
peed on him. Think I'm lying? Course I'm lying.
Say, Foster, lookee here.' Brady motioned me
to look under the table. 'What you got there, Brady?'
'Nothin' you don't,' he said, 'just lookee here.'
I looked under the table and I saw that Brady's
hand was stretched out, and I stared at it to see
what he meant."

I

"His index finger and thumb
were touching to form a circle as if he were
signaling to show me everything's okay.
'So what do you see?' he asked. 'You're not
pinching on to anything?' I asked, and at this
he started laughing, so I looked back under the table.
'Can't stop staring' at it, can ya Foster?'
'Well, what am I supposed to see?' I asked,
and he laughed and said, 'I just bet you can't
stop starin' at it.' Brady's behavior was at
its damnedest, so I sat there watching a young
couple at the next table, bent toward each other
holding hands and not speaking, even as the man
got up to push three buttons on the jukebox
to say the very thing he meant to say,
and when I looked back at Brady he had his hand
on top of the table with the thumb and index finger
touching again. 'Ha! See what I told you?
Can't stop starin' at it, can ya Foster?'"

SIOUX LOOKOUT

His father called, and Foster walked down the slope
from the nape to the shoulder of a hill.

"Look here," his father said. "Ground's broken.
The sod's been broken out and fitted back.
I can't figure it."
                On top of the hill,
the monument with half a face and arms
crumbling to the re-bar in its bones
raised a hand to shadow its eyes,
staring at the valley, a river road
where lines of Mormons crawled toward Deseret.

"Looks pretty fresh," his father said.
"Sometimes they bury herbicide out here.
Too small for a calf."
              The monument
stared at a distant tractor raising dust.
Evergreen spears of yucca quilled the flanks
of the hill, sticking to the pelts of sod
that feather as they go to seed. Mormons
waded through the valley, the riverbed a map
they called "an angel with a blazing sword"
that led them through the desert wilderness.

"Can't be more than a month old," his father said.

They cheered, mistaking the hill for the crest
that they would cross into another desert,
but the hill stood between them and more sky,
and they dreamed of being buried in the sky.

His father got down on his knees and dug.
He said, "I've got to know what's buried here."

The monument stared at the ghost of dirt
that plows broke and the wind unlocked.

13

I

"Look hard. The river's not on half the maps.
Even the wind is lost and goes around in circles.
In twenty years, this stupid wind can twist
telephone poles into cedar shapes and move
the hills around, exchanging them with valleys....

Pity the land surveyor who passed through here
marked x's down for windmills, nothing else
to hold the eye and then the windmills plucked
by storms no one remembers from the wind....

Before that came a frontier giant who
despaired at the sight and let his stick drag,
got drunk on the distance and pissed himself a river.
Soon our boat will be drunker than
that giant, staggering under the heavy sky....

Cattle can't see the river's a boundary and the stream
moves fast, contained by cedar-knotted bluffs.
Barbed wire fences come down the hill
like scars stitched into the air.
Cedars spread by bird shit make its fold
less dismal than one hundred years ago,
so downed trees bridge the river bank to bank...."

FOUR MAPS

We have three versions of the landscape,
enfolded in the deep pockets of a back-pack:
the first, a road map of towns so small their names
extend for miles beyond the city limits.

On the second map, the Dismal whorls around
like the darkest line of a finger print
that proves the river's what we say it is,
a paint-by-numbers topography:

If you color in the elevation circles
figuring in for the lack of rainfall,
the summits and the highlights,
you may see every shade of brown there is,
except this map is blue.

Legend has it that on the third map,
when you give an inch, the river takes a mile.
This map makes promises it cannot keep.
Around every river bend you'll never see
the close-ups of encaptioned birds and trees,
but at two red slashes meant to mark
two crossings, the second one called Seneca,
we hope to find a fire ring and sleep.

The fourth. On yellowed paper left to warp
on the Dismal bank, a dry spot in the mud,
we found the scribblings of a child. Either that
or someone's penciled in a river dodging
like a polygraph mapping someone's panic.
These random scribbles show us the way
to zig-zag toward a rumored crossing.

"I hope we know a crossing when we come to it.
Maybe a bridge? − or something not quite a bridge,
a landfill bottomed by a culvert, or a road
that vanishes beneath the shallow water
and comes up on the other side, continuing
to a place named Seneca, for displaced Iroquois,
who displaced Chippewa, who displaced the Sioux,
who were driven to a place that small pox opened,
the remaining Pawnee displaced to Oklahoma.
Maybe settlers from a New York town called Seneca
came here and named the new town for the old,
settling it so late that all the good names
were already taken: Omaha,
Ogallala, Brule, Dakota City.
When those names ran out, or when people forgot
or never heard the names the Indians used,
they gave the places Indian sounding names
like Broken Bow or Council Bluffs or Weeping Water,
mortal and ironic names,
or names from other places that didn't fit.
A man named Halsey built a man-made forest
and spelled his name in trees against a hill.
The river they called Dismal is not so dismal
and is hardly what you call a river."

"This river is no more a river than
the irrigation laterals we carved
into the river-bottom we rented from Brady.
The interstate was driven through that place,
along the margins of the Platte, a bit
more of a river than this because the land
around it was flatter and fitter for gravity
irrigation, though the ground wasn't much
less sandy, and so the Platte was wider.
Brady said they dug the soil up
for concrete mix so even a slicker like you
should know that it would soak up all the water
we could flood it with, and yet the holes
filled up with ground water. We called them lakes,
and they kind of were, or sandpits. Some were stocked
with fish but most were stagnant ponds,
infested with mosquitoes, algae, God knows.
In a pinch, as the lower end of the field
turned brown, the water soaking in
after crossing only half the ground,
we dropped a power-take-off driven pump
into this interstate lake beside our land.
The water level dropped ten feet a day,
and in two days we had to wait for the lake
to fill with the water we dumped on the corn."

"That Eighty was the only piece of ground
my father held on to in his sixty-odd-years —
twenty miles past the one-hundredth meridian,
the line that divides the wet states from the dry.
And so the Eighty fell under what we called
the Rocky Mountain Rain Shadow, and my father
didn't even own it, didn't own a scratch,
but rented, share-cropped, paying through his skin
the landlords, bankers, and crop-dusters, at times
renting nearly a section. But the Eighty
he rented for dry-land prices, sunk a well
and paid the utilities. A couple miles
on further east his brothers married farms
or bought them, mostly married them, and the blamed
sky rained more. Still on the Eighty, a chance good yield
was just enough to keep driving him into debt.
A good piece of land, flat river-bottom,
good for gravity irrigation like I say,
and he didn't blame it much that the winds that sometimes
seemed to bring on the smell of distant rivers
hinted at how the Pacific mists would wring
themselves dry before crossing in our direction.
Didn't blame the sky or ground but blamed
himself and worked harder."

"Even though
I was lazy with books there were times I half
admired him — stubborn man, he lived
for the spring if the banks would carry him. I was twelve
when he first stuck me on the Johnny-popper
when something else needed doing. I'd squint
up from the half-cultivated field where my
father took a stand against the dry wind
coming down the mountain. He was a giant then,
but later I thought he was a fool, but then
I worried how he judged himself as he went
into town to kick around a junkyard for piece-meal
to mend a ridger. There was a lot of time to think
on the tractor, so I asked my father what he thought about,
and he smiled. Before he lost his teeth he whistled —
still did, since he couldn't hear himself for the noise.
Every year we farmed the Eighty, and the last year
it was all we farmed. I remember the spring morning
my father woke me and told me how last night
all night he heard trees shedding ice. With the bank's
faith he felt good. Said he could smell rain
clear off in June and it'll be time now soon
and we'll get out there with a disk and plow,
we'll comb the field with a lister and go-dig,
we'll make a mark, we'll scratch up some dirt."

ABANDONED FARMSTEAD

Across the distance of contested lands
behind the shack, the draw ran true to west,
and in the shattered mud and footsteps
turning stone in the sun, the riverbed
cracked and curled into a ruin of shells.
The shack leaned with its walls still parallel.

His father floated in the water trough,
like a space man in his welding mask,
riding a windmill down through clouds of algae,
running molten beads across the cracks so that
triangles in the windmill wouldn't collapse,
worrying as his family drifted off.

He broke the arc to give his eyes a rest
as two dogs passed the house and shrank to dots,
hiding behind the blind spots in his eyes.
The rows of corn converged on the sun, and everything
aside from the sun, which swelled on the horizon,
everything, even distant memories, converged.

He saw the molten sun repair the break
between the days, but when they cooled, they cracked.
Starlight pin-pricks ached inside his eyes.
He dreamed he used his welding wand to fuse
the hinge between a shadow and a tree,
still working at a way to mend his family.

But everything he welded came undone,
the shack collapsing on its own.
Wind whistled through the windmill's skeleton.
The trough went blind with cataracts of moss.
Finally he was lost, drifting into space,
helpless, as his children left the place.

Insolvent, forced to leave himself behind
when sunlight beat the ground to smithereens,
he glanced back through the rear-view mirror,
in a car that shrank upon a shrinking road,
until the last speck of farmstead disappeared.

MOVING FROM THE FARM

Husks of corn stalks rattled with decay.
Wind ran in the rags of those old ones
who stood so long to die on their feet.
Birds watched from fence-posts,
the carved heads of walking canes.
A pie-tin on a string battered against a tree
while dogs stupid from neglect
barked at nothing.

His father walked a last time to the farmhouse,
and he picked up a coffee pot pocked by .22's,
considered the paint flakes in the grass,
the sagging porch, the windows empty,
empty of any chance to see them coming back.

"BALLADE OF THE BACK ROAD"

"My father's still in business, takes it a day at a time,
'just keeping ahead of the wolves,' he says, and goes
from Gothenburg, looking for a way to find
a deal on irrigation pipes. He knows
the man will give him credit, and he also knows
the farmer he'll deliver it to won't think
it too forward to ask for a check. 'That's how it goes,'
my father says, 'No problem. Everything touches everything

if you take it by steps. If I get to the bank on time,'
he says, 'I'll be able to cover the checks I wrote
to sell this pipe, buy lunch, drive back, not counting the dime
I'll use to call this man who maybe owes
me some. Tomorrow I'll pay off what I owe
this other guy, but maybe I'll sell something
before then, or maybe I'll take out another note,'
he says. 'No problem. Everything touches everything.

Now if you'll just help me load this load there's time
for maybe another delivery for the cash flow
to start tomorrow with.' He drives me out to find
this farmer's farm, and soon we're lost, driving along rows
and rows of corn, and my fathers says, 'I suppose
it wouldn't hurt to get to this first thing in the morning.
Let's start driving back before the gas stations close.'
He says, 'No problem. Everything touches everything.

If you leave out the middle you'll never come close
to what you're trying to get at, which in this case is gasoline.
'Seems I can't remember where this road goes,'
he says, 'No problem. Everything touches everything.'"

A BIRD
ON A
HOOK

AT THE FIRST CROSSING

Foster takes the opportunity to dig
into the garbage bag where we've stored our provisions
and pulls out binoculars that do us no good
since we can see no farther than the next river-bend,
or the hilltops, cluttered with cedars.
Then he extracts a dime-store compass,
but if there is a quicker way down the river,
the river will find it on its own.
Finally he withdraws a metal tin
with a stage painted on the lid in a frame
of purple curtains. Four shadowy dancers
are backing off the stage, and a disproportioned
green house is stage center behind the word
Opera, being more than just a label,
being a physical part of the scene, providing
in the *O* and *a* the loops to tie
the curtains back. Off-left, the shadows of
two courtiers bow to a female shadow who,
in can-cans, holds a shepherd's crook between
the two courtiers, facing each other in Rorschach
inkblot symmetry. From inside the tin,
Foster takes a piece of foil folded
over many times and unfolds it,
keeping it from the wind, and deep inside
this pouch of foil I see that there are two
minute triangular tabs of paper, each one
imprinted with a Chinese dragon. "Take one,"
Foster says. Then he takes one.

MESSENGER

We dance barefoot on fresh-cut straw
as brooms sprout up to sweep us off our feet,
amazed the river's learned to talk,
gargling with a rock stuck in its throat.
Perhaps the waters imitate the winds
that make the trees nod yes yes yes.
We wince and dance and lose our balance.

When Foster asks, "What's wind, one thing or many?"
a hard fall knocks the wind right out of me.
(Crickets tisk behind my back.)
I would say that the wind's an invisible mask,
loosely molded to fit my face
but I've lost my voice. Talking hurts.
I walk the walk of learning how to walk.

Perching in the crotch of its family tree,
a jaybird laughs to mock a crow,
the Heckle and Jeckle of a minstrel show,
does a hawk and sends the other birds rioting,
throws in a cuss word it learned from a cat,
then dives and spears my sandwich wrap,
bobs and swallows, blue scales shining.

While I stumble, trying to catch my breath,
coughing a fit to scare the bird off,
this fool's cap with a cartoon mugger's eyes,
the very malice in a patch of sky,
this mimic doesn't scare, but stares me down,
and coughs back, rasping with its tongue stuck out,
as if hacking were my solitary sound.

A WARNING

The jaybird says, "Put on your shoes
or you will know what a broom feels to sweep
and SWEEP and SWEEP-up after you!
Your words all say one thing. 'I'm HERE,' you say.
That's all I get out of you. 'I'm HERE!' As if I CARE?
So what? So what? So what? Sooooo Whaaaaat?

So why don't you listen to me once in a while?
Did you know I can pick seeds from a farmer's beard?
My grandmother was a lizard with blue scales?
You already know that? Well, did you know that
I still have a lizard's tongue? Would you like to see?
Don't you hate these nest-builders, all of them?
Aren't you tired of bullying these silent, timid birds,
cowards all, except my kin, you know them?
The jackdaws, magpies, crows and ravens?

Did you know that I once blinded an owl?
I laughed and laughed. Did you think you could scare me?
You? with your fat naked feet, and −ACK!!
You're ugly and crippled as birds without beaks!
And there's other things you LACK, you LACK!
You LACK, LACK, LACK, LACK, but I lack NOTHING!
So long as I keep my sense of malice!
Because I NEED nothing else, not even my own nest!
And I promise, before the day is through
I'll HAVE your whole sandwich!"

DRUNKEN BOAT

/Light bleeds from the sky. "Is it dawn?"
No. "Is it dusk?" No. Foster waddles to
the back of the canoe and looks in my eyes.
"Badger holes," he yells, and the valley shimmers
with his black laughter/ the Dismal stares up
at what stares down/ we're caught in its grin
whistle in the teeth/ mad similarities
portray us everywhere/ "Look at that hill!"
Foster waves his paddle. Every shadow is the dusk.
Rhythms spurt like blood that sloshes through the body.
Foster starts to pick it up/ yells STROKE!
the cedars go beserk/ yells STROKE!
I close my eyes. Who knows what passes?
Boat's a spit on the fiery water.
"Damn Presbyterian's back up on that hill
Whacha see up there buddy? Tell us somethin'!"
Keep my eyes closed/ veins in my lids map the trees.

Sit up and Foster's standing over me —
we're grounded on a sandbar Foster calls
a tow-bar now like Huckleberry would. I say,
How long have we been here? "Hours."
Hours? Foster walks to the other end,
always keeps his paddle in hand makes him
feel adventuresome and drops on all fours
mushing his face with sand and I start/
laughing & laughing & laughing/

LUNCH

The jaybird comes again to hawk for trash
and sweeps in from the woods to stand upon
our picnic table, dancing toward our bread,
puncturing the wrapper with its beak,
and, launching to a nearby limb,
bobs and swallows, unimpressed
by the full range of the human curse
as Foster swings his paddle at the branch,
surprised to see the bird swoop down at him,
making him duck and cover up his head,
heart-pounding and panicked, but surprised to be glad,
glad that he could fight against this bird for food,
glad to curse and have the jaybird cursing back.
This is what he came here for.

LOST

Mud swallows scatter from adobe nests
as we intrude into their underbridge.
Brief shade. We launch toward a grass-knitted point,
and Foster waves his paddle like he was shooing
it away and still we ram it. Foster looks back at me
as if I were working the canoe against him.

/Foster's looking extremely red to me:
red face red forearms red 'kerchief with black
paisleys yellow dime store cowboy hat
with a red hat band. We take out the map,
but we can't understand it until we climb
up the bluffs.
                              /How long we sit
I can't say, but at some time a pickup truck
comes over the hill and crosses the bridge
letting two leopard dogs out. The rancher opens
a gate and they run down to the river to get a drink
of cool Dismal water. We wave and start on toward him.

"What's this bridge called?" I ask, and the rancher shrugs
and says, "It ain't called nothing!" and so we stand
about like dupes, and I can see the rancher
has us measured up for idiots,
because confusion makes our tongues flap wild
and miss the accustomed points of articulation.
Then Foster asks, "This road run anyplace?"
And the rancher says, "Well, no place you would know,"
and stares at the distance, pushing back his cap,
seeming to wish that he were someplace else.

"So just where *is* this bridge?" I ask,
and the rancher asks me, like he never heard me right,
"You asking me where?" I nod. "Well, *here*,
where it's always been. Been here most everyday for years."
Foster drags out his map and says, "Just show us where."
But the rancher looks confused by the map,
like a man who finds himself two places at once.

Foster says,
"I thought the river alone would've taken us
farther than this, but that eternity
back there was only six miles long?
Do you suppose the river's lost? Did you know
it got off-course one night, plowing through
the pauper's graveyard of an abandoned town,
the vagrants packed in head to toe in a wedge
between the river and a road? The caskets
bobbed up and washed away, riding the flood
like six-sided canoes. When we were back
at the bridge did you notice any signs?"

DEATH OF THE JAYBIRD

On a broken fishing line,
miscast and twisted around
a cruciform telephone pole
hanging over the Dismal,
we see a jaybird spinning,
hooked through the beak.

Soon its feathers will drop
and its wings will drop
and by pieces the bird will be
carried down the river,
branch to river trunk into the ocean,
the washed-out roots
of a tree growing backwards.

"So my father was standing and looking at the sky,
but the first thing I saw was a bird like this one
hanging from a fishing line strung from the attic
door of our garage, and I said, 'What is that?'
and my father said, 'It's a warning!' 'A warning?'
'A warning for the birds to stay out of our garage!'
He left it hanging there, God knows why, for a week
before I cut it down, and I watched for something to happen
but nothing happened."

LIMBS IN THE WATER

It was a fearsome back and forth.
That river locked us in its way
and circled all around and back
to take us from behind. It spun!
I do not lie! It spun!
and sideways, backwards,
forth it dragged us under limbs.
It wished us off its back.

A barbed wire fence came down a hill
and tacked on Foster's wrist. "Goddamn,"
he cried. His wrist under water.
His blood not a feather.
"Goddamn. Goddamn."

And then it started getting dark.

Just look at him,
how he hangs to his mom
to stay on the ground,
flapping his one free hand.
Lord, I'm asking you,
do something about this.
Let him blow away, Lord.
Let him lift off the ground
and get caught in the trees.
I want to see him
bounce off windmills.
I want to see him
eclipse the sun into dead winter.
I want to see a whole flock of him
eat the light out of the sky.
Make him enormous, Lord.
Make him like harvest,
devouring the earth.
Don't let him hang there
with that one hand
flapping like a dead wing
caught from a branch.
Let him explode
like the moon explodes.
Let the snows come down,
cover up his grave.

"I've heard that photographs of folks who sleep
in moonlight fall and fracture, or fade on pianos.
I've heard that jaybirds trapped in houses
or gathered in the cedar-shade bring death
to whole families before leaf-fall.
I've heard that flowers bloom out of season
with the dying flush of old men.

Once, a babe looked into a mirror and sneezed,
and then a light snowfall fattened up the graveyard."

THE POWER PLANT

Along the riverbanks, cottonwoods bloom,
and luminous silk-strands follow the river,
sticking to the green of fireflies.
The dark wind snuffs the candles out
of farmhouses huddled alone in the dark,
and kerosene lamps flicker out to join
the jaybird swelling, blooming from its flesh,
a flickering vapor that rolls ahead of us.

We follow the bloom into a small town,
suspended in a web of power lines.
All lights join the bloom. The porch lights go out.
The neons smeared by rain go blue with cold.
In the cars all the dome lights collapse,
and blue darkness drops on the town like a dim
puppet dropped in a heap of loose string.

We see our halos glowing in the Dismal,
the current teasing our hair.
Our lips are red leaves floating out of our mouths,
floating beneath the bridge, beyond all speaking.
We slip down a tailrace to a water check,
where the boat tips over in the sway and turn.
The bloom slips under, and we're drawn after
into the turbines of the power plant.

Somewhere in a garage, where no shadows move,
and every shadow gathers in one spot,
headlights narrow their pools like a car-struck cat,
as darkness slowly enters through the eyes.

But just as everything seems lost, the moon
lifts its lid a little wider every night,
opens its dead-blue eye in the vivid air
of ozone and thunder where dreams are visible
even when your eyes shut tight.

The dynamo begins to hum again.
Darkness bends away from the light of town.
The power lines snap tight and spark,
and a puppet jerks upright with a glowing face
and prowls down a vein of light reflected in
the Dismal waters as the moon keeps pace,
bursting open on a cottonwood.

THE TIPPED CANOE

I come up for air.
               Foster, where have you gone?
The shore extends a phantom limb
as Foster yells out, "Coming from behind!"

He rides a giant salmon bare-backed,
backward down the Dismal River,
trying to bull-dog it back upstream,
a canoe that doesn't want to spawn and die.

Unable to keep up, I thrash about,
a lunatic to directions, and I yell, Foster!
Don't leave me behind!
            "Follow my voice,"
he calls for nothing.
            My heart churns
memories like a pump sucking up mud.
My life passes before me. It almost kills me
to remember each summer I passed by as a kid
ignoring the water.
            Foster!
              I remind myself
of too much and my heart is lugged down, worn
and unable to keep up with your voice,
garbled by a jaybird's racket, disappearing
in the dark.

TERMS

If I die before I wake, let me float downstream,
but not on my face. Let trees move by,
but make the moon keep pace.

"Follow my voice," Foster cries to me,
disappearing where the riverbank
and water muddy up into a blank.

And if I'm towed by any song,
please pick my shadow from the dark,
distract me from the jaybird's voice.

"Down in the dump, some tires burnin',
puttin' up a black smudge.
Somebody's fishin' for somethin' he lost,
takes a stick and pokes the rubble,
cursin' his bad luck.

A jaybird's coughin' in the cold, cold evenin'
roughs his feathers, lookin' round
and wonderin' what's he ever gonna do.
A smokin' dump so down and dismal
an owl starts weepin' just to make a sound.

Black flies are boilin', chinless rats are crawlin',
draggin' their full bellies on the ground.
A dead cat flattens as if he's still hidin'
from somethin' that got him
a long time ago.

Now up a black line, there's somethin' or other climbin'
lookin' like two catapillars, breedin' in the sun.
The jaybird dives
and somethin' snags a hold on him,
and flies start to worryin' how to get a bird down.

Down in the dump, somebody's diggin',
lookin' like a mannequin I used to know.
But a new odor's callin' him,
and he ain't even listenin',
he's quiet as a fisherman glued to his pole."

CROSSING
OVER

THE LOST BRIDGE AT SENECA CROSSING

After we gave the river a foreign name,
the Dismal brought us a plow to tilt the land
beneath the swell and diastole of moon,
uncovering fire circles, shards and flint.

For one hundred years, the Dismal clawed
at the cedar-bluffs like a man half-buried,
his heart quick with panic, digging with
the dull knife lightning lost in the water.

The valley deepened like an open grave,
and now the river searches back and forth
like a blood dog with its nose to the ground,
the moon pumping up, swollen, panting in the heat.

We hear the locusts throbbing in the trees
between us and the moon. We hear his heart
so slow we take the pulse with calendars.
The river pounds inside our chests.

Maybe the panicked heartbeat of the rain
about to be assassinated by a thunderbolt
removed the heart and left an open scar
of river stitched together with a bridge.

Our hearts beat faster, gathering in the sound
of water ruptured underneath the bridge,
but then the water rises, slurring, cuts its stitching,
and pitches down the land, escaping us.

LANDING

He climbs a hill to sulk as if he could find
a still spot, the center of the earth, the navel,
and all his feeling would be pressed into a soft *was*
— soft? Maybe like gold or maybe hard
like a kernel, immutable, never growing yet fully
mature, then Foster could draw all his feeling
from the world, and — grounded — he could draw
the lightning down, his heart beating like
rumbling tin sheets — like the sky, he thinks
— his heart beating so he can feel it in
his feet and thinks the ground's heart is a seed
and pounds like his — if this, he would never
know what it was he felt, he would only think
it was the rain he felt. If I left him standing
until morning, let him bury his feet
in the ground that feels his heart's beating until
I walked up the hill to greet him, he'd say "I am Foster's
tree and here I stand. I can do no other."

TURNING POINT AT LONE TREE

He grabs the only tree on earth before
reaching the point of no turning back.

The windmills turn, and Sandhills in their long
sleep toss and turn beneath the sod.

The tree turns, with the season, colors enough —
turns blue with empty leaves, turns cold, turns white.

The wood goes smooth where cattle turn around,
combing their hides clean on the twisted trunk.

Rain runs down the clouded branches.
Bare limbs stretch, mapping the river out.

The tree turns on its axle, turning loose
leaves and rivers that borders can't turn back.

He tries turning loose himself,
but his hand turns against him.

His knuckles turn white.
His grip to wood.

TOTEM

He opens his mouth
and says, "Once I was nothing but a mouth.
My toothless mouth was all-consumed by mouth.
The dark tongue tucked the darkness in my cheek.
But when my first tooth bit into my cheek,
my tooth was foreign to my mouth."

I

                                        He says,
"When my mother took me from her breast,
things came apart. The clock hung on the wall.
My grandfather's cup was on the tabletop.
I could not tell his snoring from the clock.
The old man on the coffee can was clothed
in a sheet woven from the sky's fabric.
The trees stood in flocks. The moon turned away.
The coyotes moaned for a lofty perspective.
My grandmother was more ancient than the old man,
but they both held the cup two-handed like I did.
Naked spools mated and I wore my clothing,
and, two-handed, I pulled myself to my feet
by the table's edge."

I

                        He says that,
growing up, he caught the lowest branch
and climbed the antlers of a cottonwood,
self-conscious of the watchful sockets
where the limbs were torn, where sometimes
watchful owls looked out, and insects ciphered,
and branches frisked him like a raccoon's paw,
a light fur on one side of the leaves
like pelts of field mice hung out to dry.

Squirrels chipped and snapped their tails in warning
and scrambled for the safety of the clouds.
Woodpeckers hammered at the tree and hollowed in
because the tree was dying. A jaybird
gave up its nest and flew so high the river
was as small as a silver hook.
                        From that height
the farm was a map he tried to memorize
before the branches could not stand his weight,
the punky wood beginning to smoke,
the animals escaping from the smoldering trunk.
Underneath the bark, he marked a map
with worms of valleys scarred by streams.
With every branch he broke, an animal got loose.
He stood on its stump with his arms out like this.

LANDLESS

Foster stands in the rain
and looks across a shadowed valley,
arms out, drenched as the new born.

He is Foster, sans profile in tree
and carries all of Foster with him,
sways and bends,
no ground to hold him —

a jaybird singing in his limbs.

"My first dead kin, my grandmother's brother,
planted the first tree in Cozad, Nebraska.
Felled for power lines, its stump was a stage
where my cousins and I danced his skeleton's clatter.
In his casket he seemed lit by his face-bones.
His heart beat so quick it could not be heard
above the humming wire hung over the graveyard.
Dressing him in his Sunday best, laying him in a cellar,
the undertaker gave me a stamp-sized Bible.
And after he told me of Lord Jesus rising
like the badgers from their winter's cave,
my cousins warned me not to sleep with my arms crossed.
But I wasn't afraid of those who hide in closets,
who wander in nightshirts, webbing the air with trees.
I stretched my arms out as if they were new branches,
then I held myself all night, mumming the dead man's pose."

I

One evening, his mother found the windows open,
the curtains drawn out by sounds the wind murmurs
under its breath, and going down to the pasture
to the lone tree, his mother saw the nightshirt hung,
flagging surrender in the clutch of carrion.
She wondered what thirst rippled through his sleep
to take him on callused knees and palms
to a field-mouse nest full of jelly-skinned young,
scratching at holes under logs rotted soft,
digging out rabbit burrows beneath bramble.
Waking to this she almost refused to claim
she mothered this one with animal stripes
welting on his legs. The clock struck
like stones. The night turned strange
as flowered walls festering with weeds and strains.
And yet she hunted the boy down to pick burrs from his hair,
to keep him from the chill of the moon-struck night.
With her coat on his shoulders, she carried him back
to a bed still wrinkled with the shape of a child.
And she stared at him until she recognized
the sleepy sounds like growls escaping from his lips,
and his animal hair, his two fisted eyes.

He sees by the light the world doesn't take.
The green tree sheds its green light so he sees
how green the tree is. And the tree is in the shape
of its leaf. And sometimes he looks in a mirror to see
how much he resembles himself and how nearly
he missed resembling the cold, flat image.
He thought he'd turn out differently.
And he is blinded by this rage

"to see myself," he says "in some other's shape,
seeing in my mother's face a part of me:
each eye, the brows, a mouth lost in a face
almost like mine, given back unlike the tree's
red light, rejected like the green light of trees."
He sees vapors in lands where it is driest. He sees age
as age when the face seems somehow young.
He sees by what seems.
And he is blinded by this rage

to see himself as a part of a whole. What takes
water to the ocean, robs him of his boundaries,
devotes us to the elements. And he wants a stake
in the all-in-all of this human mobility.
That's why he moved from a small town to the city,
hoping these same manners will work in the caged
and people-thick streets as in the half-peopled prairie.
And there he was blinded by the rage

to see himself in dim-lighted humanity
by what light was reflected from the news page.
The streets were the last place that he wanted to be,
for he was blinded by the rage.

"Class B, but in the runnin', gotta cattle-shine
on ma boots and a big smile, a little green,
hungry and open-lookin' but don't you be fooled,
I can match you sleaze for sleaze, that smile's
'cause I'm greasy as a roach smoked down about yea.
I can match anyone here for the doings
of extremity, ain't no hayseed, been hanging
between a sweet eighteen-year-old
fresh from the detention home where she
graduated, kept runnin' away until
her birthday came, ain't none of my doings,
she's excitable, fucks out loud,
I knew it when I saw her but she's gone so
how's doing? I bet your daddy's got a summer home,
and you a fur-coat that died for your sins,
just the painted woman ma mama warned me of,
but hey don't shy away, just kidding, we'll have fun,
snoot coke by the board foot, I swear, smoke joints
big as a working man's finger, no grief.
Don't hurt to be home-grown, gotta kinda
redneck chic, it's only nights like these
that make me look so hungry 'cause I'm
the underdog tonight you see the dog
outside who kinda paws the door and that
makes me every bit as dangerous as you."

But really, his mother had no voice in this.
"She refused a voice, " he says. "She kept to herself."
That's his excuse. When he asked her once
how he was like his father, she refused to answer.

Instead she kept a silence while she worked,
weaving a rug for them to wipe their feet,
strung together with a "wept," a white
and endless string, and always incomplete.

"Anything I say will be taken wrong," she said.
"If I said you were like him, you'd be mad,
if I said you weren't like him, he'd be mad,
I'm not going to say anything at all," she said.
"I know the both of you love me but that's all I will say."

Instead she made the shuttle glide across the warp
with whatever colors that crossed her mind.

His mother dances again in front of the blank
and he sees she's darker now around the eyes,
and her hair hangs like withered branches
or rampant thistle, choking off the river trees.

And whether from motion of water or clouds she vanishes,
his mother's face is resurrected from behind
the insolvent day-light: an empty moon,
losing herself back into herself,
lips blackened by dreaming.

He wishes his mother could speak just a few words,
the soft quills catching fur or cloth
but stinging not at all, even if she ached to say them.

He wants her to hold him, but darkness holds him instead.
Trees reach out over the river so far they tremble
at the flood and fall, and she receives him,
his arms stretched out to catch himself.

DOWN
THE
DISMAL
RIVER

I

A coyote woke us and Foster bolted up
from under the canoe to stand stock still
covering his eyes against the glare of the sun
and staring at the herd of cattle where he
heard the coyote yell, and then staring
at the spot where the cattle were staring
until they were all staring at the same
dip in the land, a single tree where cattle
gathered to rub their sides until the tree
grew twisted and the soil wore through to the sand,
a path leading out from the tree to the river.
In the tree a meadowlark, yellow breasted like the sun,
its wings and back a dry grass brown. The sky
was clear. And Foster stared long and stupid
like cattle staring at the spot a car honks at
long after the car has passed the spot, never
seeing the car, only knowing the noise, the origin.
Looking disappointed, Foster came back to the canoe,
and together we dragged it to the river, leaving
a long path of matted grass, and with Foster in back
we put-in.

The valley deepened, and the day
was as slender as the open sky between the bluffs.
We could hear water trickling from the hillsides,
not from run-off — it hadn't rained that much —
but from underground streams, we guessed,
because the air cooled when we heard the water,
and once we saw a bobcat and were surprised
because it was no bigger than a tom. The hills
towered over us like thunderheads, and the trees
stretched from the river to the hilltops, thick
so that though we knew that beyond the hilltops
were the rolling wastes of the near-barren Sandhills
it seemed we were in a different landscape.
But soon the river widened, the hills came down,
and the cedars that suggested a mountain forest
were replaced by cottonwoods, some toppled by
the widening river, ash-white in the sun,
naked and scarred by worm-marks looking like ciphers
from the worms that once lived beneath the bark.
Our knuckles were swollen from mosquitoe bites
from the night before — that's why we were so anxious
to be moving that morning, but with exercise
our joints were loosened and we felt like sitting,
so we tied the canoe to one downed tree and climbed
the legs of its branches onto the trunk which was smooth
and suggested the beauty and danger of submission,
and we rested.

Somewhere we had crossed a time-zone
— we didn't know where. Dragon-flies — Foster called
them snake-doctors — were also resting; some appeared
to be eating. Up-close, their mandibles fit into
their heads with such a clear seam, their heads joined
so apparently to the segments where their four wings
rotated and to the pen-like thorax, it seemed
they were skillfully cast from colored plastic.
We too ate, taking plums and muffins from the cooler
and continued down the river. The river continued spreading
and began to look much like the Platte, which is French
for flat — a good translation, Foster tells me, for what
the Indians called it, and soon we began to bottom out
on sandbars. But after a time of pushing the canoe
from channel to channel, we found by paddling
from point to point as the river meandered
we could stay to the main channel's six inches of water.

When morning passed
we saw less wildlife and much more livestock.
We floated past a farmyard where pigs were rooting
among car bodies half-buried, half-submerged along the banks,
keeping the river from robbing the farmer's land.
The pigs stared at us, mud-crusted, legs spread
to keep their mass balanced, then they scooted
up the slope as if their fear was a game.
A sow was lying on her side in a hole she'd dug
in a shadow of an abandoned school bus.
Two piglets frolicked like puppies.
We floated around another bend and saw
three barbed wire strands come down from the hillside,
disappearing in the water, but we heard them scratch
the canoe's underside and saw that they were tagged
with moss as we crossed over.

The day was like a blue-glass jar,
a little smudged by clouds but a rare find, and Foster
was about to tell me for the fourth time
about how he watched several hogs in confinement
nip at a sow and keep her running in the swimming
heat of one August afternoon, keeping her away
from the mud hole until she hyperventilated and died,
when on the steep incline of one hill we saw
three cream-white, hornless bulls, reclining
like Greek deities, under a cottonwood,
massive even from the distance we kept,
powerful, even in repose, even asleep,
they were mountainous, a whole landscape in themselves,
which peaked at their shoulders and then
rose again to their upright heads, knobbed
at the missing horns, ridged over the eyes,
which were closed. The land was theirs, entirely;
their sleep entire; they were entirely
themselves, covered in the pure blond hide
which was folded at the neck like on the necks
of huge men, but they were beautiful. One stirred,
and we were stilled as he rose on his short hind legs,
then his front legs, disproportioned to his body,
which was incredibly long. And we saw that his hair
grew long and fine on the end of his tail and was tufted
on the end of his cock. On his left flank there was burned
a valentine, a bar. He moved down the slope to where
the grass was long and never noticed us, never turned
to watch us float away, and began to feed.
The day grew wide as the river. We could see
in the distance rainbirds cluttered around a muddy pond.
Then we saw sandpits ripped from the flanks of the hill
and tall dumping bins to load trucks with sand. Behind me,
Foster said, "You see the hang on that bull?"
We floated by a car tire that had caught
a branch that caught a mess of twigs, and Foster
started talking.

"Reminds me of a bull
that Brady owned, called Athabaskin, son
of Cezon, a full-blood Charolais who sired
six years of quality carcasses. Christ,
to see him standing at pasture surrounded
by all his dams, Christ, to see him mount
again and again like there wasn't hardly time
to mount them all, and to see Brady smiling,
watching him, leaning on a post, and singing
this crazy song about how 'the Athabaskin
bastard caused the fall of the Pueblo,'
sung to the tune of *The Walbash Cannon-Ball*,
and Brady would grin like a cat eating shit because
that bull produced the most even marbled meat
you ever saw and everyone knew it. Brady
could rent the bull out for custom mounting, he called it.
Every time you'd see Brady in the bar he'd talk about
the time that rancher from Cheyenne offered him
twenty-eight hundred for the bull, or how that smart kid
just out of ag-school wanted to freeze Athabaskin's
cum and sell it to Texas. Brady said
they'd probably keep it in the state treasury,
and sure enough that bull was the most valued thing
that Brady ever owned, worth more than his car
or tractor, worth as much as an acre
of river-bottom. Take a ride with Brady
on the interstate and see a semi mounted
piggy-back on another semi and he'd say,
'Better not let ol' Athabaskin see that,'

as if the old bull would try to rival
the trucks and get himself killed. Brady claimed
that Athabaskin once got a hold of a foreign
car and almost totalled it. —God,
he was proud of that bull. Now you're a town boy and you
won't understand this but Brady loved that bull
more than he did his kids, for the same reason
that they lived in a sway-back frame house while
the barn was painted new each year. Brady
had seven kids but there was only one
Athabaskin, son of a prize bull whose cum was worth
fifty-five bucks a wad."

■

"And late night, after the bar
had closed and after Brady had ordered a six-pack
to go, we'd load up into his pickup and head off
south on highway forty-seven into the hills
that Brady called the cat-steps, probably 'cause
they were kind of terraced on the sides with small clumps
of grass that only a cat could climb, and soon
we'd take a country road that went back deep
into the hills, and then we'd leave the road
altogether and drive through canyons linked to canyons
until we passed a wind mill that ran all night long,
pumping water into a tank. And if it was winter
Brady would get out with an axe and crack
the ice and toss it on the ground, but mostly
it was summer and Brady would have no chores
and instead of stopping we'd go right up
a hill, right to the hilltop where we'd bail-out
to take a leak. Even far off, there was nothing
to hear, just the regular slug of the pump, but aside
from that there was nothing. We'd stand quiet and listen
until it seemed we'd gathered the whole land in our ears.
Brady would be walking about, pacing and squinting,
and sometimes he'd disappear over the side of the hill
for a while, but sooner or later he'd say, 'There he is.'
I'd look where he was pointing and see old Athabaskin
asleep upright as if he were watching guard, but entirely
asleep, entirely himself, the moon-light lighting up
the two bulges of his hornless head held upright
as if he too were listening, gathering in the whole land.
And Brady would say, as if we hadn't heard him,
'There he is.'"

"It was a clear day when I
was riding with Brady, checking fence lines, and Brady
saw him first, speeding up and swearing, 'Sweet Jesus
tits,' and then I saw him: Athbaskin
was squared off with a Hereford bull across
the fence and through the fence they were butting
each other but not hard and I couldn't figure out
why Brady was swearing so, until I noticed
like a fool that the Hereford bull had horns
and Athabaskin didn't. I sat inside
while Brady got out and started walking toward them
until his smarter side stopped him, turned him back
until he stopped again and turned toward them
and turned back and finally stood in one spot,
stamping, 'Holy Holy Holy Holy.' Then Brady
got back inside and we were moving toward
Athabaskin until we butted against the side of him
because Brady meant to move him down the fence line,
but the pickup killed and after Brady started it,
the wheels spun in one place and Athabaskin
started to butt the harder. So finally Brady
backed-up, revved the motor and — slam! — hit
Athabaskin broad-side and down he went.
Over the smashed hood I couldn't see Athabaskin
anywhere, and the other bull had run off
and stood some thirty feet away, looking at us.
Brady screamed, 'Jesus, sweet Jesus, that's
what I get I've gone and killed the bastard,'
and he got out and looked at the bull
which was lying on his side for maybe the first time
in his life, then Brady started banging on
the pickup as if the bull hadn't done enough damage
to suit him."

"But the bull was breathing short breaths,
and after a moment he rolled to his stomach
and managed to find his feet and stood there
for a full ten minutes and then lay down again.
We sat there in the pickup and watched him
and for three hours he did not move.
Then he stood up and walked to the salt-lick
and lay down beside it and did not move.
And all this time Brady repeated to himself,
'That ain't right that ain't right somethin's
gone wrong with him,' and something was because
after that Athabaskin had no interest for
any of the dams that Brady brought him.
And Brady went so far as to buy these
strange exotic dams he'd heard about that exude
an odor that can bring a bull from miles away.
They were nothing to Athabaskin. Finally
Brady loaded Athabaskin up and took him
to the packing plant, not a big packing plant
where the workers wade in blood to their ankles
and use rods that shoot a metal pin into
the cattle's head like they have in Omaha,
but the local one in town beside the meat locker.
The killing floor was just a single pen,
and though Athabaskin seemed quite gentle
the workers elected the youngest and quickest
to go inside with a .22. At the first crack
it seemed Athabaskin woke up. The kid
came flying over the fence with Athabaskin
following, and when the bull hit the side of the pen,
which was made from rolled steel, it buckled.
Then Athabaskin proceeded to make shambles of it
while the kid sat on one side and shot him
four more times before the bull dropped.

The kid laid down the gun, said he fuckin' had it
and quit then and there, while the old guys
stood around laughing a little, kind of nerved.
Brady thought about the consumer
unlucky enough to buy that bull's tough meat."

"Brady's got himself a new bull now, one of those
new type Simmental-breeds that were first imported
back in '71 and that the university's found to produce
higher-yielding carcasses. He went out to a sale
and bought it, the top-selling bull, a son of a
BH Cruzeiro 90 and out of a BH Cruzeiro 6 bred dam
and weighing 1,325 pounds by the name of Axion
2980 — Brady's pride would accept no less.
And that bull will try to hump anything he sees:
haystacks, metal Quonsets, he don't care what.
Brady just shakes his head as if it's a bit
too much to handle and tries to joke, saying
he's afraid this bull will break through the fence
and head toward the Rockies. And sure enough,
his wad is worth a bundle, and Brady's selling it
to a rancher down in New Mexico. Brady
doesn't know how it's done. Some company
does it for him. Brady says he'd rather not watch."

THE ACT OF WATCHING

We leave a wake I cannot see that on
the upper reaches of the river does
not dissipate but reaches shore and makes
a sucking sound as waves lap underneath
a ledge of grass, a sound like muskrats clucking
that often makes us look for life when it
is only rhythm for our passing. Now,
our wake swells out. The water parts and closes.
The wake swells out and dissipates.

TO THE RIVER'S MOUTH

"The corn fields of my home stretch on
further than my eye sees. They are deeper than
my seeing memory, three maybe four generations.
But their brief life may end with me: the land,
the dusty old dust my forebears orphaned—
unknowing, my parents pushed the land up in a whirl
of plows and even the land leaves the land
in the end. And there's no new world.

As we clamor to keep the land alive we've gone
to building monstrous anhydrous ammonia plants.
Have you heard of them leaking? Well, they can, and lawns
will fry, and people's lungs will burn, and plans
to evacuate these small Midwestern towns
don't exist. This ammonia's a fertilizer, but leaves curl
and brown at its heavy touch. It is toxic for humans.
At our journey's end, there is no new world.

I want to know if this is the time when our waste overcomes
our promise, when the ghost-dust of our wasted land
will blow about our ankles, broken from
the cycle of life. Our water recedes from us, the stands
of trees whither, aquifers fall away, and we stand
here waiting for foreclosure, the quick rural
ending that the creditors demand
at our journey's end, when there's no new world.

Grandfather, when your children brought you to this land
in your old age, they never planned
to plant you close by, just so you could see them
end up where there's no new world."

THE NEXT BRIDGE

When we came to the next bridge we put out
— burnt tender and skin thick from mosquito bites,
bitten by barbed wire and scratched by trees.
With an old hand pump, we took turns
dousing each other with water over the head.
Foster thought he was lucky, thought he had
preserved himself, but as he stepped from the boat
his bare foot found a barbed wire buried in mud.
So the Dismal took a bite of him at last,
and he limped around and cursed. I washed his wound,
and he washed mine, which made me look a kind
of animal, a strange one, red stripes,
blistered, and bipedal. Then Foster said,
"My father took me to a man-made lake
that blanketed a farmer's land, and then
we saw it again, this time on a tree —
a jaybird snagged and twisting on a hook.
I said, 'That's three times. What's it mean?'
He said, 'It means if you leave a hook out,
you're gonna catch-on something.'"

The Dismal hooks around without us thirty miles
then joins the Middle Loup at Dunning, Nebraska,
joins the South Loup, Loup, and Calamus,
joins the Cedar, then becomes the Platte
and is still the Platte when it joins the Elkhorn
but is swallowed by the Missouri at Plattsmouth,
joins the Little Nemaha, Nishnabotna, Big Nemaha,
Tarkio, Nodaway, then swallows another Platte,
joins the Kansas going through Kansas City,
joins Locust, Chariton, Lamine, another Cedar,
joins the Little Niagua at Bonnot Mills,
joins the Gasconade at Gasconade,
goes through Creve Coeur and on to St. Louis,
joins the Mississippi, Kaskaskia, and Ohio,
passes Indian burial mounds,
joins the Ohion, joins the Hatchie,
joins the sewer waters coming from Memphis,
joins St. Francis, Arkansas, Big Black,
and the river where the Red and Black
and Atchafalaya join. Now many rivers
woven together join the Tompson,
the ooze of the dumpster joins and widens
with the iridescence of the motor pools,
and somewhere near here Huckleberry said,
"We began to come to trees with Spanish moss on them,
hanging down from the limbs like long grey beards.
It was the first time I ever saw it growing,
and it made the woods look solemn and dismal."

THE RIVER'S MOUTH

We've gone from the city to the river's mouth
and back, but what now? Do we sit down and wait,
giving up wanting to eat the world all at once,
and do we consider the damage we've done?
Do we consider this? This gulf bitten out?
The teeth marks on all beaches of the world?
All the buildings crumbled on one side as if
the sun were rotting them? —These do nothing
to stop the famished aching at the sight
of hedges, roses, all the bleeding colors
breaking out between the buildings. Oh, man,
what can we do to stop this hunger? My gums
are receding. My gums are plenty bad.
Trench mouth's what this once was called: soldiers
looked out from the trenches and bled at the sight.
—Imagine the bleeding acres they surveyed!
I've also heard this called "vicarious menstruation."
We bleed at the sight of the world, we want
to bleed like the world, but all this bleeding's bound
to take my teeth away. Let's get moving again!
We must not stay here long enough to taste
the putrid water, red from rusting pipes,
or tongue the missing teeth of vacant lots,
or see the curtains sopped, inflamed by sun,
a drop of blood that's swallowed by the ground.

A HOOK

Since then, nothing's caught my eye except
the Monument to Thunder Mountain.
I pulled the car onto the shoulder and couldn't
stop starin' at it: behind a fence
someone shaped a totem out of fiberglass
and chicken wire pressed together with bits
of malformed animals, looking more like
a boy-scout project than a totem shaped
by Indian scouts. The sun had bled its color off
which once had been, I guessed, outlandish,
clashing with the landscape's many shades
of brown. A billboard painted with stencil
lettering spelled out the *Scouts' desire*
to acknowledge native customs now long past,
a Monument to Thunder Mountain, the small butte
across the road, not indicated by the map,
bearing no resemblance to the monument —
a holy mountain, worshipped in former times
as a dwelling of mighty animal spirits.
The young climbed the hill for their dreams
to become the foster-children of the first
animal they'd see after days of fasting:
coyote, white wolf, badger, rattlesnake,
prairie dog — the course their lives would follow—
and reading this I saw a Charolais bull,
trotting to the fence-line, challenging my car.

THAT NIGHT

I dreamed Foster climbed up Thunder Mountain
by a riverbed that dried-up years ago.
The first hard rain washed him back to town,
where neon spilled across the damp cement.
The next night he drank so late that waking
on the rock face he found the dew gone to sweat
and soaking through his sheets and blankets.
The third night, rocks began to dance down the slopes.
The fourth night, the air thinned.
The farms disappeared beneath a cloud.
For heat, he fed a fire paper-scraps
a snow fence strained from a river of air.
The short-winded fire panted just to breathe.

When he saw me climbing up the other face,
glad to see him, otherwise depressed,
still ready to witness something new,
he promised nothing, and I expected it.
But before the timberline, the sterile mountain cap,
we saw goats with horns grown back on their skulls
that drove us head-long down the mountain in our own dust,
racing to see who could tell about this first,
laughing to see which one could tell the better lie.

THE BETTER LIE

When the cartographer came to this withered branch,
believing ground would give up wheat and corn
like sighs of relief, he found a land so flat
it'd map itself until your knees got weak.
The cranes spelled seasons. The earth spoke badgers.
The run-off backed-up by leaf-fall alone.

Taking a drink to steady his hand, he drew
an illustrated map, with a seed of sun
swollen and red, about to pop into the ground.
In this story-land of Bible metaphors,
he hung a jaybird on a knot of cedar trees,
standing for the good thief crucified beside the Lord,
clutching the bluffs in the promise of paradise.
The sassy-thief he lynched up on a telephone pole.
The third among them was the owl
that lived for three days underground.

Before he was finished, but after he was drunk,
he wrote "Dismal River" down the common trunk —
from the water's source, a culvert with a golden tongue
that he named, with a flourish, "Penis *de la Patrie*"
to the cities hung on river branches,
like corpses hanging from the family tree.

TREATY

But I want the river's lost puzzle-piece
locked back in the land. I want new boundaries drawn:

a river's often pushed beyond its banks,
and its memory's too rich in debris.
I don't want lures in trees.

I want a map that keeps the treaty's words:
all unclaimed land will remain forever yours
until wind becomes the river's ghost.

RON BLOCK

says this of his family background and schooling:

"From the age of twelve to twenty-six I spent my winters in school and my summers working for my father, first doing farm work and then building and selling livestock working equipment. Although *Dismal River* reflects the deep and abiding influences of my father, who in local terms is 'a real character,' it is a largely fictional work. Only the river itself, threading through the Sandhills north of my hometown, Gothenburg, Nebraska, is wholly real. My mother taught English and reading in the public school I attended. From her I learned how to read, and she has always been interested in my poetry.

"After receiving a degree in English and Linguistics at the University of Nebraska, I spent a winter in New Orleans, helped my father build a rodeo arena over that summer, and then went to Syracuse University where I took an M.A. in English Literature and Creative Writing. I developed a special interest in the long narrative poem and in persona poems (particularly those of Galway Kinnell and Margaret Atwood). I also took a strong interest in Richard Hugo's poems of place, and I was lucky enough to be one of Hayden Carruth's first university students. He taught me how to use form as a unifying as well as a liberating device, permitting a wider range of voices in the poem.

"I'd have to say that writing is an obsessive activity, often performed when I should be doing something else. If I tell my friend Vanessa that Frost said poetry is a 'stay against confusion,' it sounds like a flimsy excuse to get out of going dancing. But then, if I didn't have people like her, my friends, or my family to read my poetry, I wouldn't write."

Mr. Block also has an M.A. in telecommunication/film. He currently teaches at North Dakota State University in Fargo. His poetry has appeared in *Prairie Schooner, New Letters, Iowa Review, Epoch,* and other literary magazines. One of his ballades from *Dismal River* was included in Philip Dacey's anthology, *Strong Measures: Contemporary Poetry in Traditional Forms.* He is currently at work on a novel.

Though the long poem has a somewhat baffling history in the twentieth century, we feel that Ron Block's *Dismal River* escapes the usual problems of disorder and confusion and emerges as an extraordinary example of the form, one of the best we've encountered. *Dismal River* is his first book.